Ask me

Which bug uses a torch?

Creepy-Crawlies

Contents

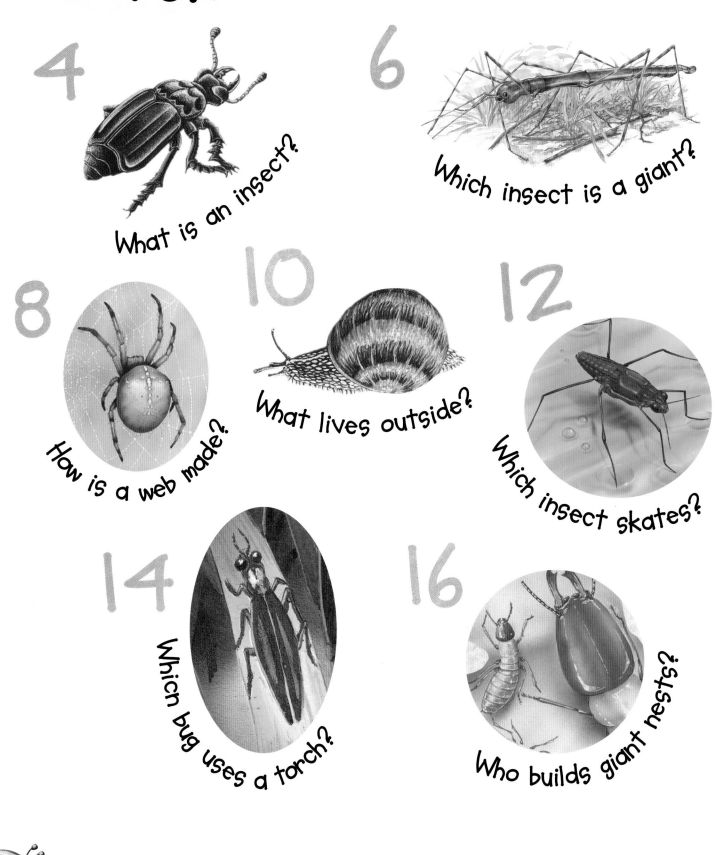

What is an insect?

An insect is an animal with six legs and three parts to its body. Its head has a mouth, eyes, and long antennae—also called feelers. Its body is protected by a hard outer case. Most insects also have wings.

Is a spider an insect?

No, it belongs to a group called arachnids. A spider has eight legs; an insect has only six. A spider has two parts to its body, and it cannot fly.

Dragonfly

Housefly

Monarch butterfly

Ant

Ladybug

Cabbage white butterfly

Grasshopper

Violet ground beetle

Which bug has over 100 legs?

A centipede. The name means "one hundred feet." However, not all centipedes have 100 legs. One kind has 350 legs— 175 pairs of feet!

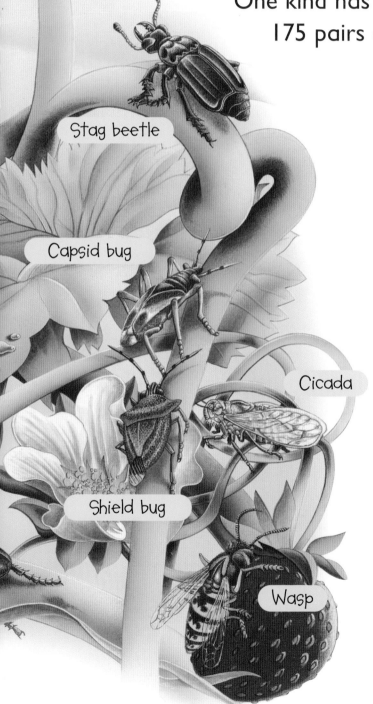

Stag beetle

Capsid bug

Cicada

Shield bug

Wasp

→ **Insect skeletons**

An insect does not have bones inside its body. Instead, it has a hard outer covering that covers its soft body and protects it from harm.

Which insect is a giant?

The giant stick insect is the longest insect on Earth. It is about the length from your elbow to your fingertips! It has a long brown or green body and legs that stick out at different angles. It looks just like a twig. This makes it very hard for hungry birds to see it.

Which butterfly is a handful?

Queen Alexandra's birdwing butterfly. With its wings fully open, it measures 28 centimeters (11 inches) across. Its huge wings make it the world's biggest butterfly.

Which insect is the smallest?

The world's smallest insect is a wasp called a fairy fly. This tiny animal is smaller than a pinhead. You would need a magnifying glass to see it. Twenty fairy fly eggs could fit into one butterfly egg.

↑ Extra-strong

Beetles are very strong for their size. A rhinoceros beetle can carry a load 850 times its own weight. That's like you giving seven elephants a piggyback ride.

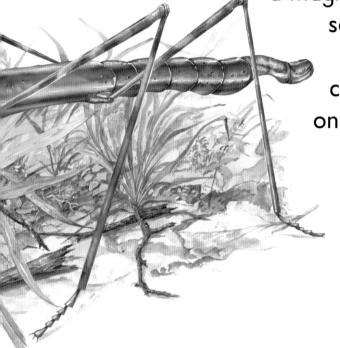

? True or false

Some insects look like giraffes.

True. An odd-looking insect called a giraffe weevil has a long neck like a giraffe. No one knows why it has such a long neck.

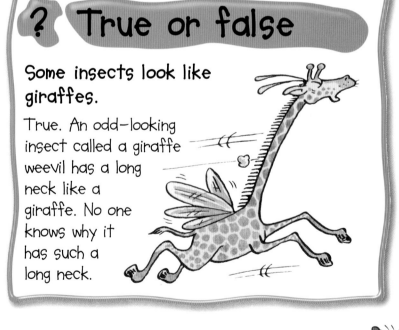

→ Longest earthworm

The longest earthworm can grow up to 6 meters (20 feet) long—that's as long as four bicycles. Imagine digging one up in your yard!

How is a web made?

Spiders spin webs out of silk. The silk is made inside the spider's body. The spider squeezes out thin silk threads through spinnerets in the end of its body. The spider uses a thread of silk to swing through the air and weave its web. The silk is runny to begin with, but turns hard in the air.

Food trap
Spiders build webs to trap food. The web is sticky, so if an insect flies into the web, it gets stuck. The spider wraps its prey in silk threads to eat later.

Where might a spider live in a shoe?

A wandering spider found in Brazil likes to hide in people's shoes. It has a very poisonous bite. One tiny drop of its poison is enough to kill a mouse.

8

? True or false

Spitting spiders spit over their enemies.

True. Spitting spiders do not bother to spin webs to catch insects. Instead, they spit a sticky substance all over them. Then the spiders quickly move in to deliver a nasty bite that kills their prey.

Which spider is the size of a plate?

The gigantic goliath bird-eating spider is huge! Including its long, hairy legs, it measures 28 centimeters (11 inches) across. It lives in the South American rain forests and comes out at night to hunt for insects, small birds, and mammals to eat.

What lives outside?

You will find lots of creepy-crawlies outside. Look in your yard or in a park. If you lift up a stone, you may see spiders, ants, slugs, worms, and centipedes. Always put the stone back carefully.

Which beetle turns fog into water?

Snail

Millipede

Garden spider

Wood louse

The darkling beetle from the Namib desert in Africa. It sticks its bottom up in the air. Fog from the sea turns into dew on its back and runs down into its mouth.

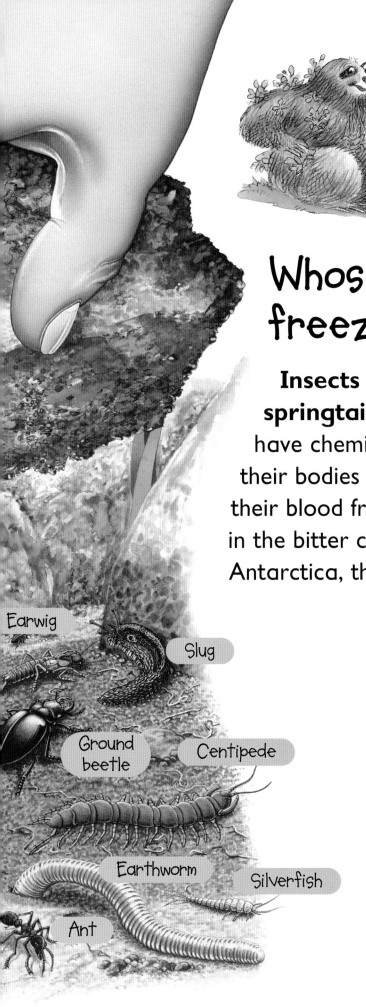

Earwig
Slug
Ground beetle
Centipede
Earthworm
Silverfish
Ant

← Home, sweet home

Sloths are so dirty that tiny green plants grow on their fur. Some creepy-crawlies also live in their fur, such as beetles, fleas, and plant-eating moths.

Whose blood doesn't freeze?

Insects called springtails. They have chemicals in their bodies to stop their blood from freezing in the bitter cold. These tiny insects live in Antarctica, the coldest, windiest place on Earth.

↑ Mountain spiders

Jumping spiders live on Mount Everest, the world's tallest mountain. It is the highest place that a spider has ever been found.

Which insect skates?

The pond skater! This insect looks as if it's walking on water. The pond skater has pads of waxy, waterproof hairs on the ends of its legs. The pads help it to stay on top of the water as it darts across. The pond skater needs to move quickly to catch its food. It eats other insects that fall into the water.

Where do spiders live by the sea?

Marine spiders live along the seashore in Australia and New Zealand. At low tide, they hunt for food on the beach. At high tide, they hide in their burrows. They weave a silk door to keep the water out.

12

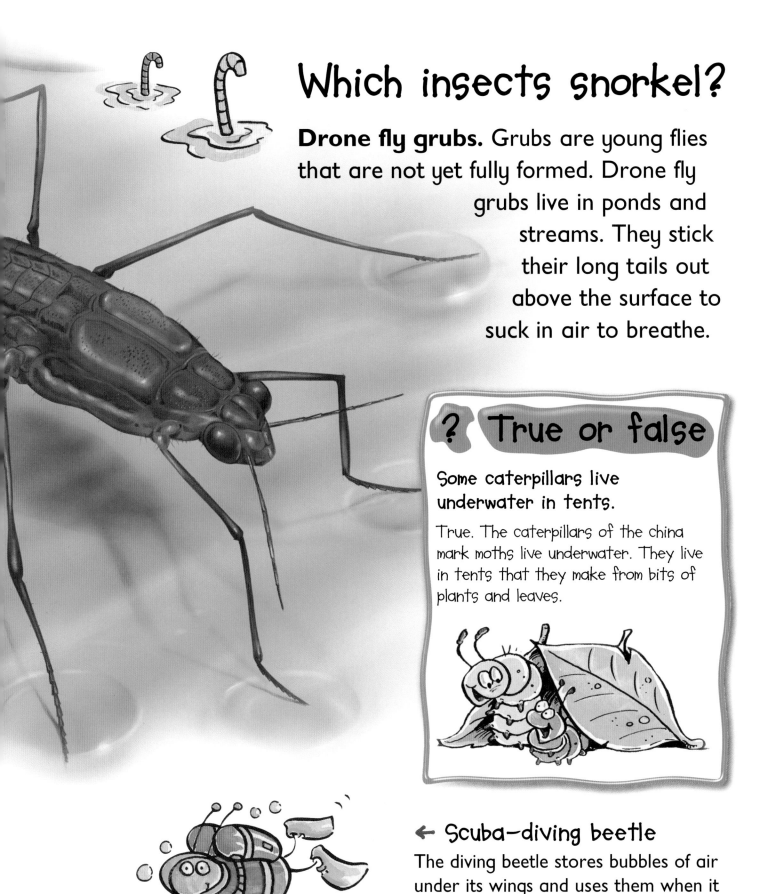

Which insects snorkel?

Drone fly grubs. Grubs are young flies that are not yet fully formed. Drone fly grubs live in ponds and streams. They stick their long tails out above the surface to suck in air to breathe.

? True or false

Some caterpillars live underwater in tents.

True. The caterpillars of the china mark moths live underwater. They live in tents that they make from bits of plants and leaves.

← Scuba-diving beetle

The diving beetle stores bubbles of air under its wings and uses them when it swims underwater. Then it comes up tail first for more air.

Which bug uses a torch?

A female glowworm shines in the dark to attract a male. She cannot fly but sits on the grass and flashes out a message with her tail. Then she waits for a male to fly by and answer. Glowworms are not worms at all, but are a kind of beetle.

↑ Can you hear me down there?

A cricket does not have ears on its head. They are on its front legs instead. Its ears are tiny holes with skin stretched over them.

Can insects taste with their feet?

Yes! Butterflies, bees, and flies taste with their feet. When they land on food, they use taste organs in their feet to tell them if the food is good to eat or not.

Why do insects need their feelers?

An insect uses its feelers to pick up smells. Feelers also help insects to feel their way around. An insect's feelers are on its head and are also called antennae.

Moth

↓ Amazing eyes!
A fly has very special eyes. It can see upward, downward, backward, and forward all at the same time. This is why flies are so hard to catch.

Do you know?

1. Where are a cricket's ears?
2. Which insect lights up?

Answers: 1. On the front of its legs.
2. A female glowworm, to attract a male.

15

Who builds giant nests?

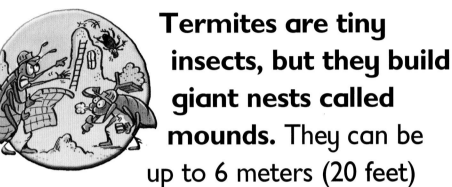

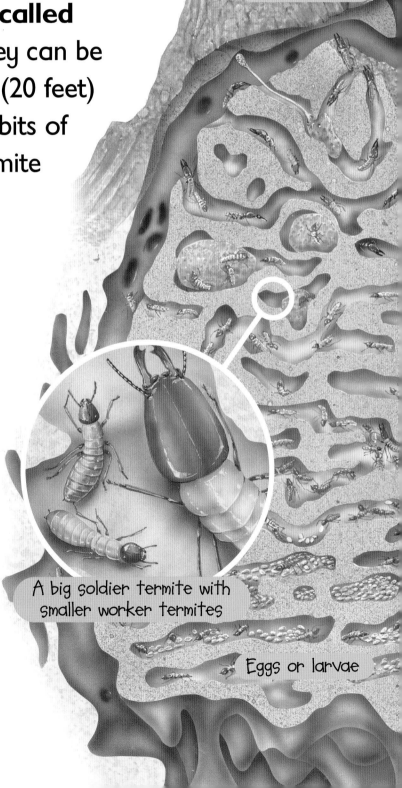

Termites are tiny insects, but they build giant nests called mounds. They can be up to 6 meters (20 feet) tall and are made from tiny bits of mud stuck together with termite spit. Millions of termites live inside—some mounds are at least 50 years old.

Ground level

↑ Spit and paper
Some wasps make their nests out of papier-mâché. They chew up strips of wood to make paper and mash it together with dollops of spit.

A big soldier termite with smaller worker termites

Eggs or larvae

Mound maze

Inside a termite mound is a maze of tunnels and rooms. The queen has her own room. Big soldier termites protect the mound against enemies, usually ants.

Food store

Queen termite

Where do baby scorpions ride?

Baby scorpions ride around on their mother's back to keep them safe. They travel like this until they are old enough to look after themselves.

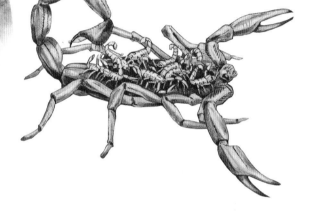

? True or false

Dung beetles lay their eggs on a leaf.

False. Dung beetles roll up balls of animal dung and lay their eggs inside the dung balls. When the babies hatch, they have lots of dung to eat!

What is a caterpillar?

It's a baby butterfly. Butterfly babies do not look like their parents. Their bodies have to go through amazing changes over many weeks before they are fully grown and look like a butterfly. Here you can see how a butterfly grows. This special way of growing is called metamorphosis.

↓ A long childhood
Many insects take a long time to grow up. Some cicadas take 17 years to grow. Then they change into adults, lay eggs, and die, all in a few weeks.

1. Laying eggs
A female butterfly lays her eggs on a leaf.

2. Hatching out
The eggs hatch into caterpillars.

3. Eating lots
The caterpillars munch on the leaves and grow very quickly.

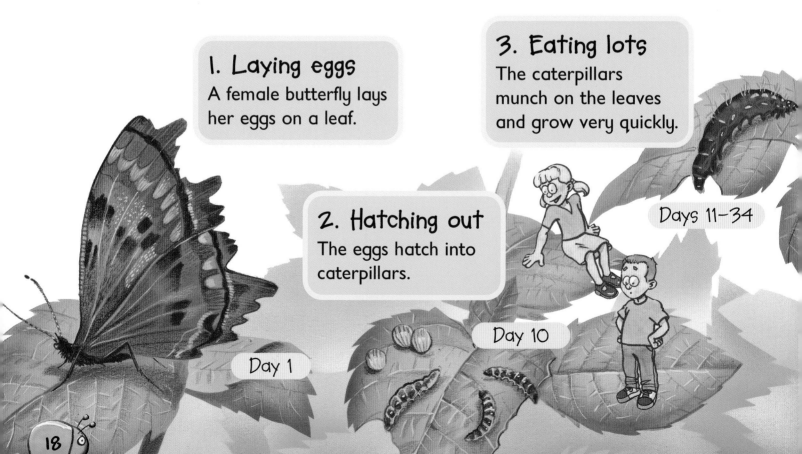

Day 1

Day 10

Days 11–34

18

What is a nymph?

A baby dragonfly. A dragonfly lays its eggs in a pond or stream. The eggs hatch into babies called nymphs. As it grows, a nymph looks more like an adult. Then it sheds its skin, and the adult comes out.

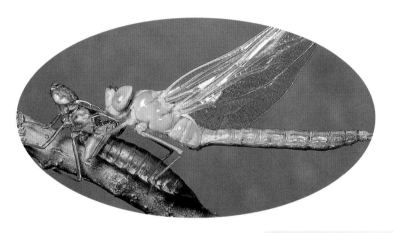

? True or false

An adult insect lives for years and years.

False. Most adult insects do not live long. Mayflies may spend two to three years as nymphs, but they live only one day as adults.

Day 50

5. Flying out

Inside the pupa, the caterpillar changes into a butterfly. The pupa splits open, and the butterfly flies out.

4. Hanging out

Each caterpillar makes itself a hard case, called a pupa.

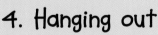

Day 35

19

Is a butterfly a fly?

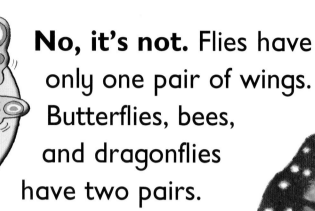

No, it's not. Flies have only one pair of wings. Butterflies, bees, and dragonflies have two pairs. Insect wings are all shapes, colors, and sizes. They are crisscrossed by tiny, hollow tubes that make them strong enough for flying. Many butterflies have brightly colored wings with bright shapes and patterns.

Monarch butterfly

Bumblebee

Heavy flier
Bees should not be able to fly because their body is too big and heavy for their light wings. But they can fly very well.

Flying record
Monarch butterflies fly from Canada to Mexico every year—that's more than 3,500 kilometers (2,175 miles)!

Which insect zooms?

In Australia there is a dragonfly that can whiz along. It can reach a top speed of 58 kilometers (36 miles) an hour. This means it could overtake a galloping horse!

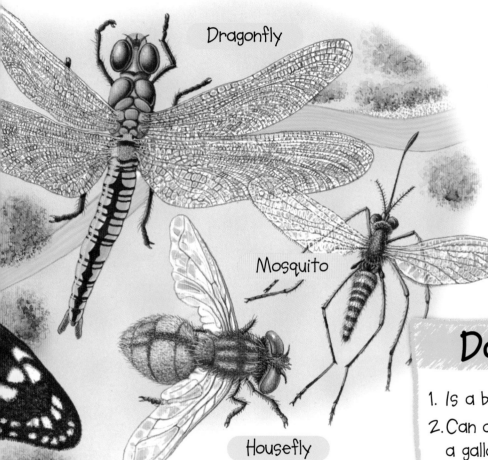

Dragonfly

Mosquito

Housefly

Who is humming?
You can tell when a mosquito is nearby by the humming sound it makes. Its wings make this noise because they are beating so fast.

Do you know?

1. Is a butterfly a fly?
2. Can a dragonfly fly faster than a galloping horse?

Answers: 1. No. 2. Yes, some can.

← Singing wings
Some male grasshoppers sing by rubbing their wings against their legs. They sing to attract females.

Which insects jump?

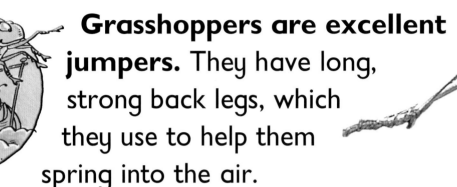

Grasshoppers are excellent jumpers. They have long, strong back legs, which they use to help them spring into the air. To escape from enemies, grasshoppers push themselves up with their back legs and leap into the air from where they're sitting.

Long jumpers

Some grasshoppers jump about 20 times their body length. Human long jumpers leap about five times their body length.

When do bees like to dance?

When they find food, bees fly back to the nest and dance. This dance tells other bees where they can find the food.

22

Can spiders fly?

They don't have wings, but they do fly.
When some baby spiders hatch, they spin a long silk thread. The baby spider hangs onto the thread and floats off on the breeze to find a new home. They can travel far like this.

? True or false

Some ants march in huge armies.

True. Swarms of army ants march through rain forests, eating anything that gets in their way. An army may have as many as 1½ million ants.

→ Cockroach racers
Some cockroaches are world-record runners. They can sprint along at speeds of about 5½ kilometers (3½ miles) an hour—that would be like you running as fast as a racing car.

Who eats the carpet?

Carpet beetle babies. Carpet beetles lay their eggs in carpets. The tiny, hairy grubs that hatch out are called wooly bears, and they chew holes in the carpet. While they are eating the carpet, woodworm could be eating the furniture. Woodworm beetles hatch inside furniture and chew tiny holes to crawl out.

↓ Tearful moths

Some tropical moths have very unusual diets. They drink tears, usually from animals such as horses, pigs, and deer. But they will also drink tears from humans.

Carpet beetle eggs

Carpet beetle

Wooly bears

Which spider fishes?

The net-casting spider. This spider spins a small, strong net of sticky threads. It holds out the net in its legs. When an insect passes, the spider throws the net over it and traps the prey.

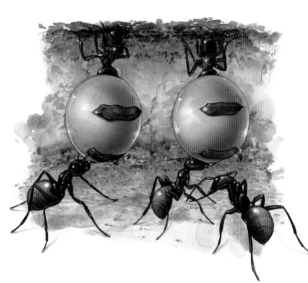

Which ants are fat?

Some honeypot ants eat so much honey they swell up. They cannot move, so they hang from the nest roof. When the other ants get hungry, the honeypots squeeze out honey for them.

Do you know?

1. Which insect gets fat?
2. Which insect eats furniture?

Answers: 1. A honeypot ant. 2. Woodworm.

25

Who fires a gas cloud?

Bombardier beetles spray their enemies with a cloud of hot, stinging gas that they fire from their bottoms! The spray makes a "pop" sound, like a gun going off. This type of beetle is an excellent shot and can swivel its bottom around to get a better aim. It can let off up to 500 shots at a time.

Which baby lives in a bubble?

Baby froghoppers. The babies group together and make a clump of white bubbles to cover themselves. The bubbles protect them from being eaten or drying out in the Sun.

26

Which insects froth at the mouth and smell?

Lubber grasshoppers, when they are in danger. They froth at the mouth to make their breath smell terrible. The grasshopper can't fly away from its enemies, but its smelly breath keeps it safe.

← Forward roll

If a click beetle lands on its back, it just does a somersault onto its front again. It arches its back, then flips over with a loud "click."

↓ Hissing handstands!

One type of cockroach scares off its enemies by doing a handstand and hissing loudly.

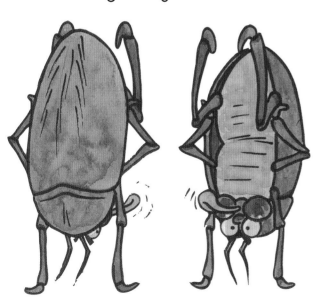

? True or false

Weevils fall off twigs if they are scared.

True. If a weevil is in danger, it drops off its perch and falls to the ground. It lies very still without moving and pretends to be dead. This is so that its enemies will leave it alone.

Which insect has petals?

The flower mantis has wings that are shaped like petals. It looks and has the same color as a flower so that it can catch other insects to eat. When another insect comes along, it will land near the mantis because it thinks it's a flower. The mantis then pounces on it and eats it.

Who's there?
The insects in this picture look just likes leaves and flowers. The praying mantis looks like a twig. The butterflies look like leaves.

Flower mantis

Praying mantis

Indian leaf butterfly

Why are some insects invisible?

Some insects are the same color as their surroundings. This makes them look almost invisible, and their enemies can't see them. This is called camouflage.

↓ **Spider droppings**
Some spiders look just like a bird dropping lying on a leaf. No wonder their enemies leave them alone!

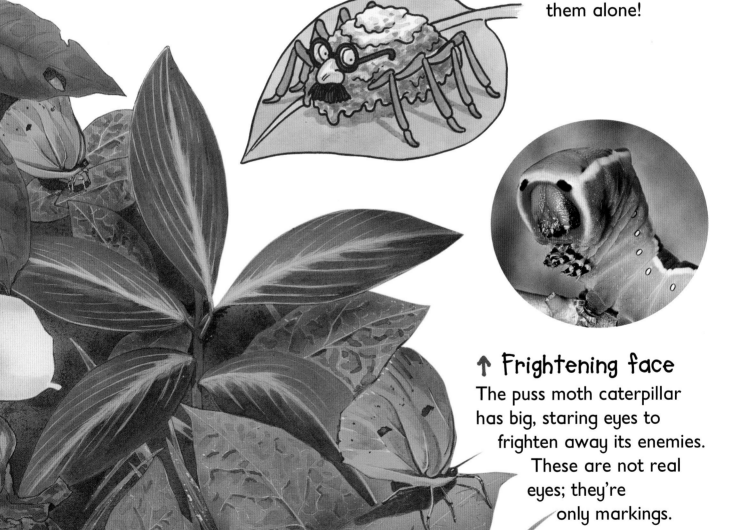

↑ **Frightening face**
The puss moth caterpillar has big, staring eyes to frighten away its enemies. These are not real eyes; they're only markings.

29

Do insects help plants?

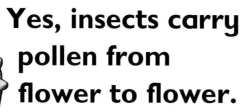

Yes, insects carry pollen from flower to flower. This helps more plants to grow. Bees visit a flower to lap up nectar. While they are sitting on the flower, they get covered in pollen. They then carry this pollen to the next flower. This flower uses the pollen to make seeds that grow into new plants.

Which insects can make people ill?

Mosquitoes are tiny insects, and some of them can make you ill. One kind of mosquito can spread a dangerous disease called malaria. Others can give you a nasty bite.

Which insects can cause a lot of damage?

A swarm of locusts. A swarm is many millions of locusts that eat huge amounts of food every day. If a swarm attacks a field, it can eat the whole crop in a few minutes.

→ Hungry ladybugs

Gardeners love ladybugs. These insects help to protect garden plants by eating the greenfly, which harms plants.

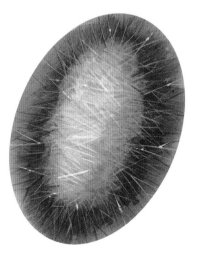

↑ Silken insects

Silk is made by silkworms, the caterpillars of silk moths. We use the same silk to make cloth.

? True or false

Some people collect worms.

True. Some people keep worms in a wormery, which is a container filled with soil. Others enjoy an unusual hobby known as worm charming. They try to make worms come out of the ground by jumping up and down and making a sound like rain.

Index

This edition updated and published in 2011
4 6 8 10 9 7 5
The Southwestern Company
Nashville, Tennessee
© Southwestern Company 2002, 2005, 2010

ISBN 978-0-87197-518-8

Miles
KeLLY

SW Southwestern

Produced by Miles Kelly Publishing Ltd
Harding's Barn, Bardfield End Green, Thaxted, Essex,
CM6 3PX, UK

Publishing Director: Anne Marshall
Designer: Warris Kidwai
Assets: Lorraine King, Cathy Miles

Printed in China

Project Director, UK: Fiona Greenland
Editorial Director: Mary Cummings
Managing Editor: Judy Jackson
Copy Editor: Carolyn King
Production Manager: Powell Ropp

The publishers would like to thank the following artists whose work appears in this book: John Butler, Steve Caldwell, Jim Channell, Andrew Clark, Mark Davis, Kuo Kang Chen, Andrew Clark, Peter Dennis, Heather Dickinson, Richard Draper, James Field, Nicholas Forder, Chris Forsey, Mike Foster/Maltings Partnership, Terry Gabbey, Alan Hancocks, Richard Hook, John James, Emma Jones, Tony Kenyon, Aziz Khan, Sue King/SGA, Kevin Maddison, Janos Marffy, Debbie Meekcoms, Helen Parsley, Rachel Philips, Jane Pickering, Neil Reid, Terry Riley, Pete Roberts, Steve Roberts, Peter Sarson, Martin Sanders, Mike Saunders, Sarah Smith, Studio Galante, Rudi Vizi, Mike White, Paul Williams, Peter Wilks.